The editors would like to thank
BARBARA KIEFER, PhD,
Charlotte S. Huck Professor of Children's Literature,
The Ohio State University, and
PAUL L. SIESWERDA,
Aquarium Curator, New York Aquarium,
for their assistance in the preparation of this book.

Visit us on the Web!
Seussville.com
rhcbooks.com

Educators and librarians, for a variety of teaching tools, visit us at RHTeachersLibrarians.com

Library of Congress Cataloging-in-Publication Data is available upon request.
ISBN 978-0-679-89116-1 (trade) — ISBN 978-0-593-81412-3 (lib. bdg.)
ISBN 978-0-593-12680-6 (ebook)

MANUFACTURED IN CHINA
53 52 51 50 49 48 47 46 45 44
2024 Random House Children's Books Edition

Wish for a Fish

All About
SEA CREATURES

by Bonnie Worth
illustrated by Aristides Ruiz

The Cat in the Hat's Learning Library®

Random House 🏠 New York

I'm the Cat in the Hat,
and I hear that you wish
to go down to the sea
and to visit the fish.

So please climb on board
S.S. Undersea Glubber.
It is made to dive deep
out of very thick rubber.

It will take us down deep—
deep down under the sea.
We will start at the top
and go deep as can be.

The top parts are sunny.
The bottom parts black.
We'll go to the bottom
and then we'll come back.

Sunny Zone,

Twilight Zone,

Dark Zone,

Abyss—

the Trench at the bottom
you won't want to miss!

Sunny Zone—sea level to 660 feet

The Sunny Zone is
where our sea visit starts.
Most of our sea life
is found in these parts.

The law of the sea
is the same as on land.
I'll call it the food chain
so you'll understand.

Big fish eat smaller fish
and so on until...
you get down to
one of the tiniest—
krill.

If you're wishing for fish,
there are lots of them here.
I see herring and mackerel
swimming quite near.

THING 1

MACKERE

HERRING

SUNNY

PERCH

COD

CATFISH

Fish can lay eggs.

They have fins and fish tails.

And most fish have bodies

all covered with scales.

These scales, they are coated

with slippery slime.

The slime keeps out germs—

at least, most of the time.

13

Fish open their mouths
and they let water in.
That's when the gills' job
really starts to kick in.

Gills sift through the water
and pull out the "air."*
They help the fish find
all the "air" that is there.

(*Oxygen, really.)

15

AURELIA

COMPASS

The jellyfish is
a most interesting fella.
He looks kind of like
a transparent umbrella!

SUNNY

ZONE

COMB JELLY

Stay away from his tentacles
(those long stringy things).
They stun prey by giving off
hundreds of stings!

THIN
2

CYANEA

Of the hundreds of kinds
of sharks in the sea,
we only have time now
to visit with three.

The six-inch-long dogfish
(no, it never barks),

the fifty-foot whale shark
(the Mack truck of sharks)—

and what have we here?

19

It is called the great white
for its white belly, great teeth,
and great big deep bite!
A shark grows its teeth
in neat rows in its face.
When the front row wears out,
the next row takes its place.

Shark bodies are made
of the same kind of stuff

SUNNY ZONE

as your ears and your nose—
that's what makes them so tough.
The stuff is called cartilage.
It folds and it bends.
And when it is torn,
the cartilage mends.

21

What else can we see
in this nice sunny water?

Oh, say, see the manatee
and her calf daughter!
SUNNY ZONE

Manatees are mammals
like you and like me.
They have lungs
and give milk
to their babies, you see.

23

Another sea mammal
we'll see is the whale.
It's the largest of mammals
we'll see, without fail.
The great whale family
is split into two:
toothed whales
(like the orca)
and baleen
(like the blue).

TOOTHED

BALEEN

Baleen fills the blue whale's mouth like a grill.
As water flows through it, it strains out the krill.

The blue whale weighs tons, maybe ninety or more. It's bigger than even a big dinosaur!

25

These toothed whales are orcas,
and few can defeat them.
They like to hunt seals
and to catch them and eat them!

NARWHAL

The narwhal's one tusk
sticks out like a horn.
It looks so much like
a one-horned unicorn!

All whales hold their breath
when they dive down below,
and when they come up,
let it out with a blow!

RIGHT WHALE

27

Before we go deeper,
let's all wave hello
to our mammal pals, dolphins—
that's them down below.

A dolphin can see
in the night—wonder why?
Echolocation.
It works like an eye.
It sends out a click
and the click bounces back.
And the sound of that click
helps the dolphin keep track
of where it is going
and which fish is where
and whether some foe,
like a shark, might be there.

Shake hands with the octopus.
Isn't it great?
With arm after arm just
for hugging. Yikes—eight!
Dear Dick and sweet Sally,
tell me, what would you think
if I told you the octopus
shoots out a dark ink?

It squirts out the ink
in some enemy's face
and then swims away
to a much safer place.

Twilight Zone—660 to 3,300 feet

Of all of the fights
that are fought in the sea,
there's one that is biggest,
if you're asking me.

Do I hear you asking?
(I'm so glad you did!)
It's sperm whale
versus giant squid!

30

Like all whales, the sperm
whale must come up for air.
But this one can dive
and then stay way down there
for two hours or more—
at three thousand feet—
shopping for giant
squid to eat.

Dark Zone—3,300 to 13,200 feet

Get out your flashlights.
It's dark way down here!
The fish may look funny—
but please have no fear!

The gigantura and
the big-mouth eel.

The whipnose,
which comes with its own
rod and reel.

FLASHLIGHT
FISH

Down here it is always
as black as the night,
so many fish here have
their very own light.
They use it to locate
a mate or some prey.
Food-hunting is hard
like this, day after day.

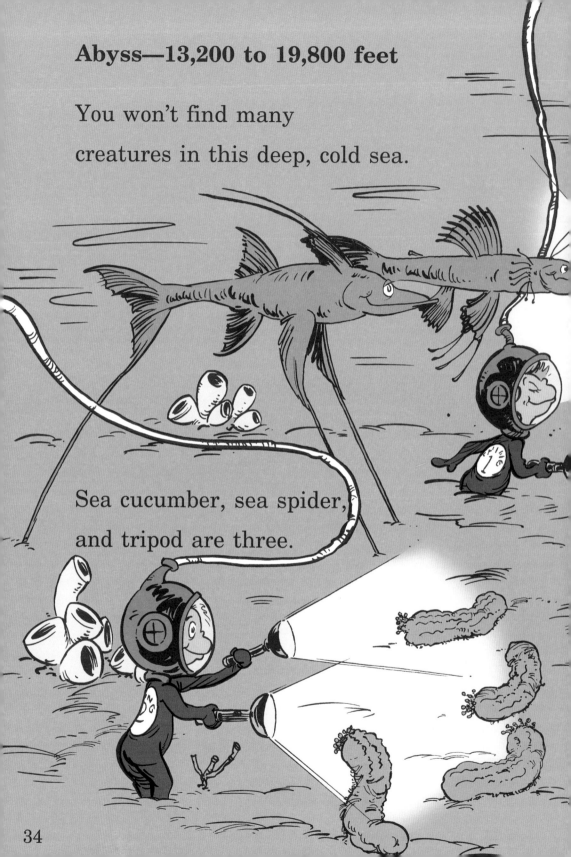

Abyss—13,200 to 19,800 feet

You won't find many
creatures in this deep, cold sea.

Sea cucumber, sea spider,
and tripod are three.

34

The Abyss has a carpet
of thick, yucky muck.
Animals have legs so
they will not get stuck.

Trench—19,800 feet and deeper

Before we go up,
it is really a must
that you visit the vents, which
are cracks in Earth's crust.

It is up through these vents
that the hot waters spout
and warm up these clams
and these worms here about.

Giant clams and tube worms
have enough things to eat
because this deep spot
has unusual heat.

Oh, say, can you see
by my undersea clock—
it is time the fair Glubber
got back to the dock.

And now that our trip
below sea is all done,
I will bet that you two
have a wish for some...

GLOSSARY

Abyss: A hole almost too deep to measure.

Defeat: To beat in a contest.

Foe: Enemy.

Locate: To find.

Lungs: The two sac-like organs mammals use for breathing.

Oxygen: A gas that is found in air. Oxygen is also found in water and in rock. Animals need oxygen to live.

Prey: An animal hunted for food.

Stun: To shock or cause a person or animal to lose its senses.

Transparent: Something so light that you can see through it.

Trench: A deep ditch.

Tusk: A very long animal tooth.

Versus: Against—a word used to describe two people or animals that are engaged in a contest.

LEARN MORE WITH THESE FUN ACTIVITIES

Visit your local aquarium!

Aquariums are home to all kinds of ocean wildlife! What type of fish can you spot at your local aquarium? If you can't visit an aquarium in person, you can watch livestreams from the Georgia Aquarium at georgiaaquarium.org/webcam.

Make an ocean in a bottle!

With your imagination and a glass bottle, you can visit the ocean anytime! Add some sand to the bottom of the bottle. Next, add some water and blue food coloring to the bottle. Put some small ocean animal toys or seashells in the bottle. Close the lid tight. Now you have your own mini ocean in a bottle!

Recycle plastic!

Did you know that millions of pieces of plastic go into the ocean every year? Plastic is life-threatening to ocean animals. You can help by recycling! Do you have a recycle bin at home? How about at school? If not, see if you can get one. Spread the word about the importance of recycling by making posters or talking to your friends and family.

INDEX

Abyss, 9, 34–35
aurelia, 16

baleen whales, 24, 25
big-mouth eel, 32
blue whale, 24, 25

cartilage, 21
catfish, 13
cod, 13
comb jelly, 17
compass, 16
cyanea, 17

Dark Zone, 9, 32–33
dogfish, 18
dolphins, 28

echolocation, 28
eggs, 13

fins, 13, 15
flashlight fish, 33
food chain, 11

giant clam, 37
giant squid, 30, 31
gigantura, 32
gills, 14–15
great white shark, 20

herring, 12, 15

ink, 29

jellyfish, 16–17

krill, 11, 25

mackerel, 12
manatees, 22–23

narwhal, 27

octopus, 29
orca, 24, 26

perch, 13

right whale, 27

scales, 13
sea cucumber, 34
sea spider, 34
seals, 26
sharks, 18–21
  bodies, 21
  teeth, 20
slime, 13
sperm whale, 30–31
Sunny Zone, 9, 10–29

tails, 13, 15
tentacles, 17
toothed whales, 24, 26
Trench, 9, 36–37
tripod, 34
tube worm, 37
Twilight Zone, 9, 30–31

vents, 36

whale shark, 19
whales, 24–27, 30–31
whipnose, 33